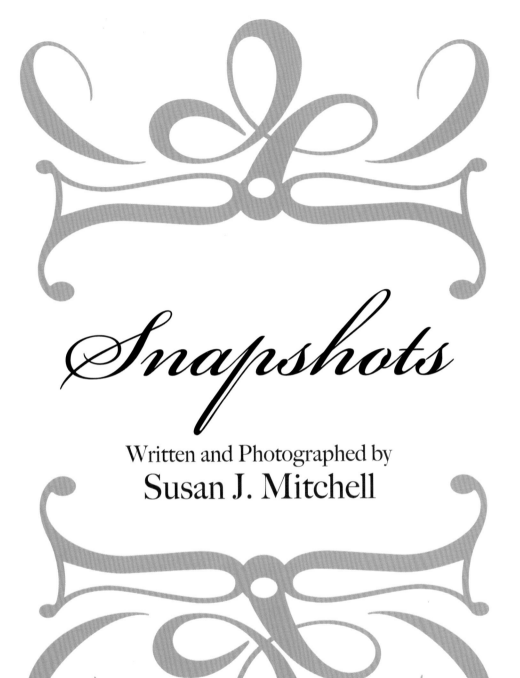

Snapshots

Written and Photographed by

Susan J. Mitchell

Heart to Heart   *Publishing, Inc.*

Heart to Heart Publishing, Inc.
528 Mud Creek Road • Morgantown, KY 42261
(270) 526-5589
www.hearttoheartpublishinginc.com

Copyright © 2012
Publishing Rights: Heart to Heart Publishing, Inc.
Publishing Date February 2013
Library of Congress Control Number: 2012951997
ISBN 978-1-937008-21-5

Senior Editor: L.J. Gill
Editor: Patricia G. Craig
Layout: April Yingling

Printed in USA

First Edition
10 9 8 7 6 5 4 3 2

Heart to Heart Publishing, Inc. books are available at a special discount for
bulk purchases in the US by corporations, institutions and other organizations.
For more information, please contact Special Sales at 270-526-5589.

Dedication

To my sister *Jennifer*,
who inspired this book.

Susan B Mitchell
December 2012

Introduction

It was the wheelchair that did it, made me angry. It was not being able to talk, to think like I used to, to feel normal emotions. It was the fact that I could not see out of my right eye. It was the broken bones that encased the broken spirit and injured brain. It was the entire world that looked different and I could not find my place in it. It was the car accident in 1995 that changed everything about me and how I would lead my life from that moment onward.

It was the brilliant psychologists and doctors and family and friends and strangers who nourished my mind and body then gave me back my soul. They are the ones who cried when I was not looking, sat with me while I sobbed, and pushed me until I wrote things more painful and strengthening than any physical therapy I have ever had. They showed me this new world in front of me and let me decide how to navigate it.

Then, in 2009 I decided to stop writing. This endeavor I had begun in high school in the 80's. It was my creative outlet, my way to figure out life when it was going well and when I crashed into it. I just stopped. Words did not have the same meaning as they did before. I picked up a camera and decided I would never write another word.

But she would not let me. She, who had taunted me as a child by following me around wanting me to play with her dolls when I had more important things to do. She, who remembers the play I wrote as a young teenager and watched as I lead my puppets in their first real performance. She, who left home to go to college but called me often and answered my calls just as frequently. She, who is a second Mom to my son. She, who saw both my son and myself after the car accident, after I died and was brought back to a life I no longer understood. She who watched me progress from bed to wheelchair to crutches to cane to my own two legs. Jennifer, my younger sister, did not accept my retirement. She did not accept it at all.

So, she reverted to her childlike ways: she became annoying. For months, she emailed and mailed to me writing competitions, calls for entries, writing prompts. I politely said, "No, thanks." She, not so politely, kept sending them and calling me about workshops, conferences. Sometimes she made suggestions, other times she was more fervent in her coaxing. I would tell her that I was putting my energy into photography. I did not want to write any more words.

One day she called me with that tone in her voice. "Just listen to me," she said.

I sighed and waited, preparing in my head yet another way to say no and hopefully she would give up soon.

"Pictures are worth a thousand words, right?"

"Yes," I said hesitantly.

"What if you take pictures and write a hundred words? Just a hundred words. You could write a book titled: '100 pictures, 100 words'."

"What about?" I asked.

"I don't care," she said.

Hmmm.

You are about to read the first installment.
Don't tell *Jennifer* I listened.

Snapshots

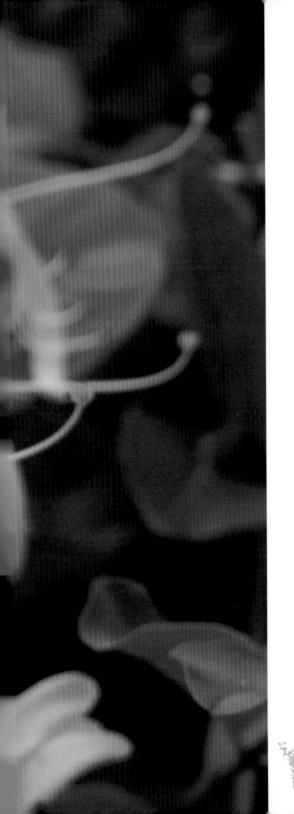

I bring this to you, this *honeysuckle*.
To you who deserve to share such a
delicate moment.
Not one caught by the lens,
but a moment in the life of something other
than yourself. A life surrounded by and
encompassing beauty just by being *alive*,
by allowing the sun the gentle privilege of
awakening it every day and saying
thank you with a soft fragrant kiss. I give
you the opportunity to take part in another's
life and experience a space in time that
requires nothing more than

your attention to what is being

said when no

words

are

spoken.

Some areas of my *life*
are surrounded by *block walls,*
beautiful gates
and filled with weeds of abandonment. I go there
sometimes and look inside, remembering the
good times
within those walls and the people
who shared them with me.
The entrance has been closed by
time, circumstances, life events.
Maybe it was closed by my own actions.
But someday, when sitting on the outside
becomes too much and the
good memories
stir me to action,
I will pick up the phone
or write the letter that will
open the gate and begin the process
of clearing out the weeds.

Some people are like the *morning dew*.
They come into your life when it is at its darkest.
Their new perspectives provide
the moisture that cleanses and freshens.
Then, when the sun begins to shine
on the darkness and turns up the heat,
they are the buffer against
burning or drying up and withering.
These people come in so quietly and naturally that
sometimes their impact isn't noticed,
especially at first. But they cover a lot of ground
and feed everything they touch
with healthy drops of *hope* and *inspiration*.

Look around.

Who is the morning dew in your life?

It is almost impossible to be totally alone where no one can see us. Nearly always there is someone who finds us *interesting*, someone who believes we are worthy of watching if only for a moment. The motive, most often, is merely a fascination with *human nature* and nothing ulterior. The watchful eye is either learning, observing or admiring. It is an educational endeavor as when we have the opportunity to see a child's first steps or an elderly couple strolling along hand in hand. *The moment is moving and makes us better for having taken the time to observe.*

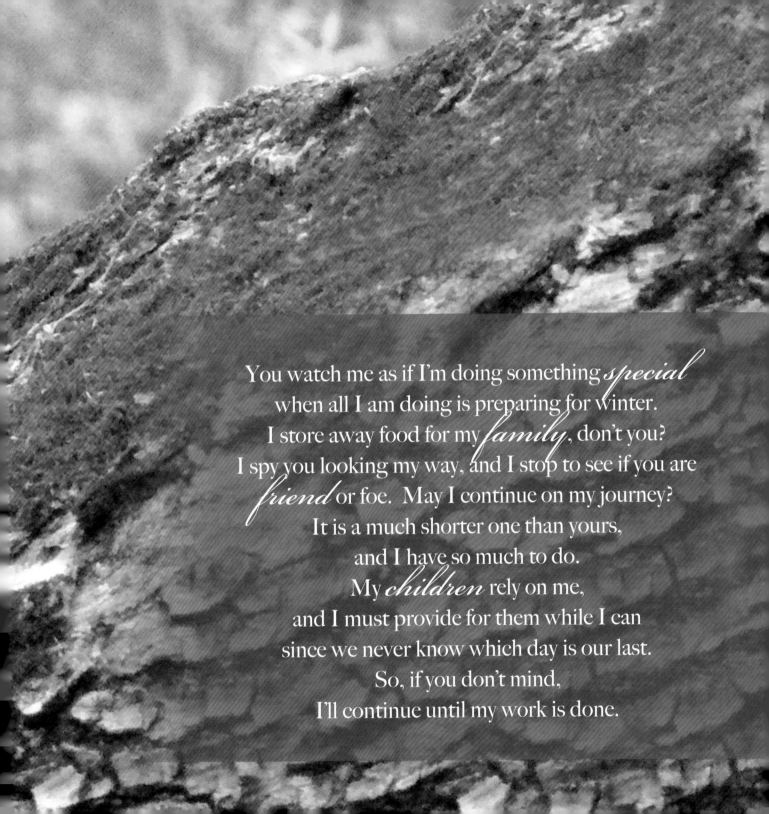

You watch me as if I'm doing something *special*
when all I am doing is preparing for winter.
I store away food for my *family*, don't you?
I spy you looking my way, and I stop to see if you are
friend or foe. May I continue on my journey?
It is a much shorter one than yours,
and I have so much to do.
My *children* rely on me,
and I must provide for them while I can
since we never know which day is our last.
So, if you don't mind,
I'll continue until my work is done.

There's calmness in *nature*.
It is a quiet without words, but it is not silence.
Hear the shadows stretching across a path, tired
leaves letting go and gliding to the ground,
bees searching for that last bit of nectar.
Lean against a tree and feel its *welcoming sigh*.
Smell the earth around you.
Taste the flavor of morning glory in the air.
Wrap yourself in the conversations of blue jays,
red-headed woodpeckers and brown squirrels.
Wash yourself in warm, clean breezes that
bathe your skin and clear your mind.
Stay as long as you like.
No one here will mind.

Life is an artist making imprints on our soul.
What some call scars,
others might call etchings.
The scars on our heart, mind and body
are teachable moments that reveal how we arrived
at this place in the world.
They are the artwork that makes us who we are.
Our greatest *challenges* have marked us
indelibly with strokes of the same pen
that created our finest attributes.
What we learn from our past is the
curriculum for our future and the future of those around us.
That knowledge gives
us the paint brush poised
above the canvas
of our lives.

Sometimes we find ourselves *waiting* at the door in anticipation of someone's return. No matter our age, disposition or path in life, we don't always understand why the person is gone or why they aren't coming back. The logic of the universe never quite explains the ache in our *hearts*, the usefulness of our *emotions* or how to make the *pain go away*. The tears don't bring them home. At some point, we must concede that neither our apologies nor our negotiations will help. But it doesn't keep us from looking out the window or hoping for just one *miracle*.

Families are made of different types of *people.*
They look, think and act differently. Each person is an individual with many
variations of likes and dislikes. People may be related by genes,
commonalities or simply by a love for each other.
How they came to be is not as important as the fact that they do.
Family is more than names on a paper tree.
It includes the depth of the connection and the *strength* of the *bond.*
Family is more than the language spoken.
It includes the words unsaid yet heard, *understood* and *appreciated.*
Family is who you *choose.*

Having money, a nice house and
a good car is *pleasant*,
but having someone *greet* you
with a smile and look you in the eye
without any demands or expectations
(except maybe "come walk with me")
can be all you really need at this *moment*.
A different perspective
– you may want to stop and smell the
roses while they stop and smell the fire hydrants –
can lead to a new understanding of what is
truly important.
Sometimes a walk around the block
can teach us we do not have
to like all the same things
to enjoy each other's
company.

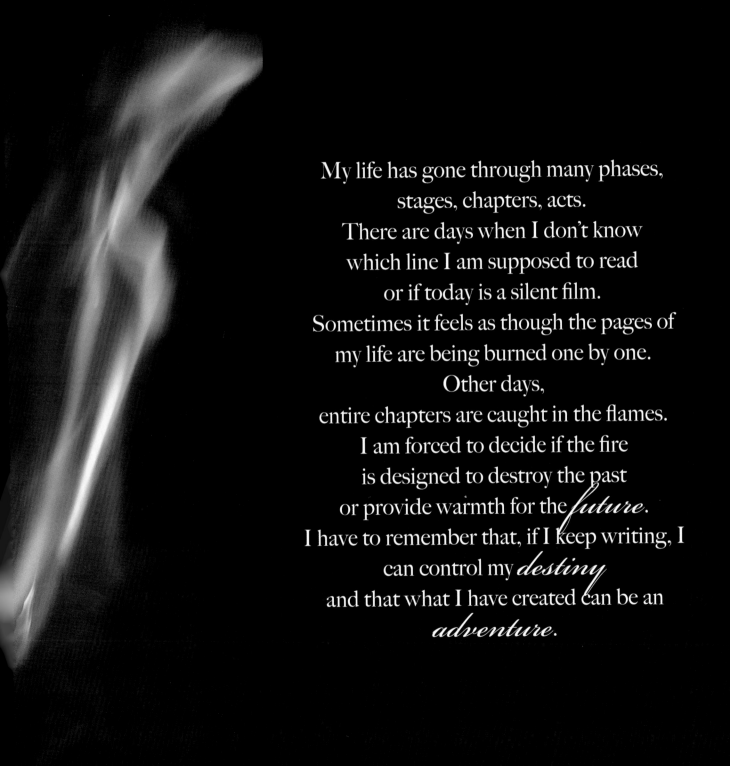

My life has gone through many phases,
stages, chapters, acts.
There are days when I don't know
which line I am supposed to read
or if today is a silent film.
Sometimes it feels as though the pages of
my life are being burned one by one.
Other days,
entire chapters are caught in the flames.
I am forced to decide if the fire
is designed to destroy the past
or provide warmth for the *future*.
I have to remember that, if I keep writing, I
can control my *destiny*
and that what I have created can be an
adventure.

Marshmallows are the taste of *summer*,
a fire its music, and frogs the chorus.
Darkness is a backdrop to mingling *stars*.
Once the marshmallows have been roasted,
the moon and the fire become focal points.
Afterward, no one needs to utter a word while
they listen and watch from front row seats as
the *earth* and its creatures provide world-class
entertainment. You know the show is about
to end when the light rises from the east replacing
croaking with chirping. The next show begins
as color pours itself across the horizon, dropping
onto *a new day* the smell of morning.

There is a *special* bond between *mother and son*, a connection without words. Even during times of anger and disappointment there is the knowledge that something deeper exists, something stronger. Sometimes it takes space, time and maturity on both our parts to realize how incredible, resilient and special this relationship can become. Once we let go enough to see each other more clearly, the connection can be one, not of chains and weights, but of freedom and acceptance. The process of letting go, holding on, and teaching and learning never ends and can make the bond a positive *lifetime experience.*

Relationships are complex.
Individuals are so many different things to each
person in their lives.
Love is a complex emotion that encompasses
a *beautiful* collage of *feelings*.
How to express your love
is just as strategic a decision as *when*,
especially for first-timers.
But, when the moment arrives and you have no
idea what to say, the best thing to do may be just
to sit down and say absolutely *nothing*.
Moments like this can prove beyond any doubt
that the words you cannot utter
are whispered on the breeze and
draped across the *memory*
of the one you *love*.

How do you describe the
color blue to a blind person?
Is it soft like a blanket or fluffy like a pillow?
How do you explain humming
to someone who has never spoken?
Do you let them touch your
chest to feel the vibration of
happiness?
Can you describe *contentment*
to an anxious person?
Is it warm like a summer creek
or lingering hug?
Can you describe second *love*
to someone who has
never experienced their first one?
Does it feel like familiar sheets
and jazz music in the wee hours?
Can you explain *life* to
someone who hasn't lived?

It is good to reflect on the day,
the incident,
the moment without dwelling
on what might have been
... if only we had done this
or if only we had said that.
Reflections without ifs are
learning experiences that color our world
in elegant, tolerant, respectful ways
so we can grow
to reflect the *beauty* of the world around us.
Leaving the "if onlys"
to lie on the ground
and decay will help move the process
and our lives *forward*
to reach their proper future.
The body of water we stare into
can change if we could just *smile*.

Nature found a way to prop open the doors
with weeds, mud and rocks too late.
Inside there's a hollow, coolness.
The exterior is worn and unattractive
but the concrete blocks are
stoic proof of its former *usefulness*.
It had purpose in its early days.
As the years passed by
so did its guests until now it stands
unremembered.
Promises to come visit have been *forgotten*
as life's twists and turns changed priorities.
It wasn't meant to be this way:
pieces missing,
future and past all muddled *together*
with no clear division.
Where is everyone?
Wait.
I hear someone coming....

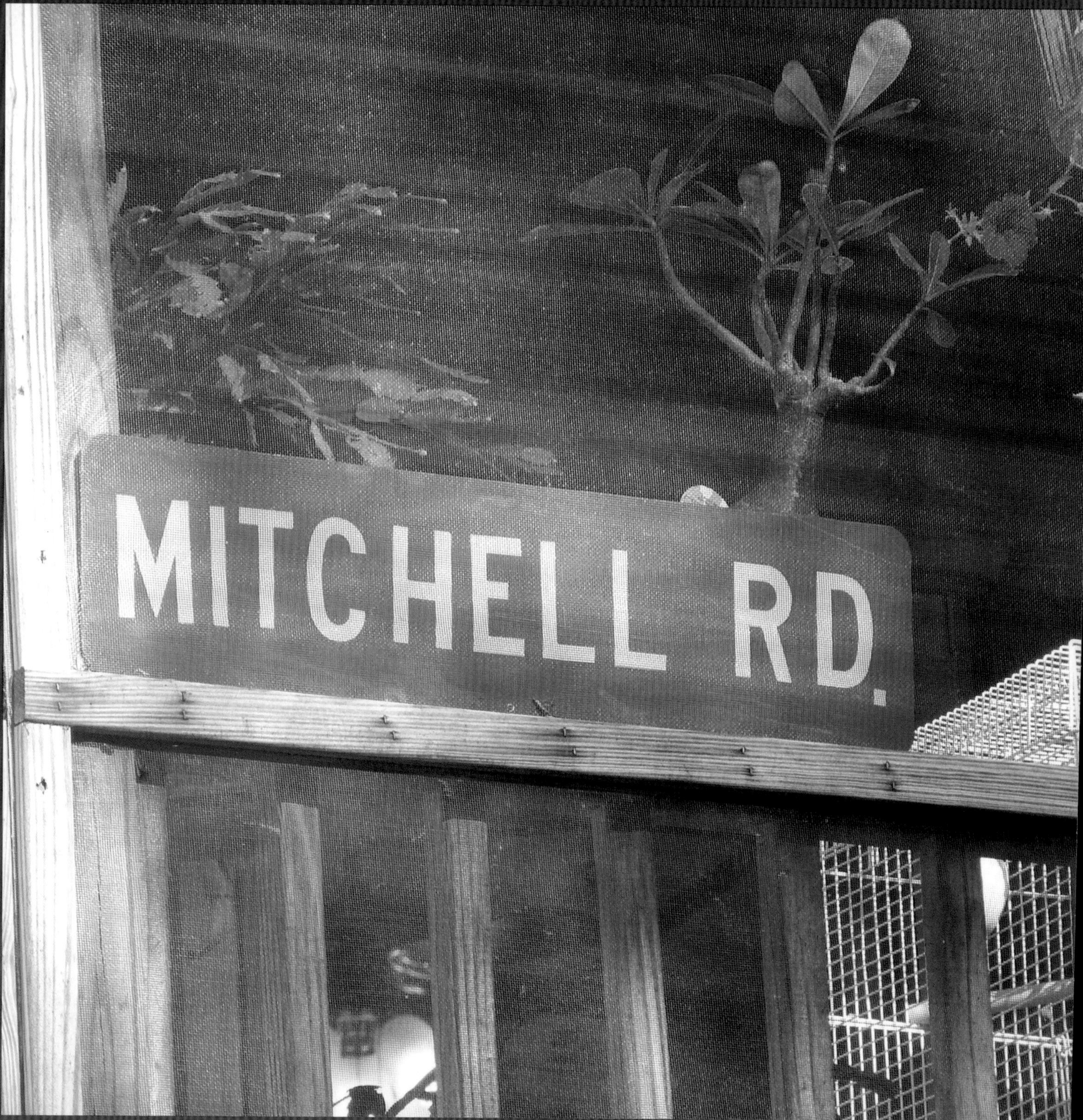
MITCHELL RD.

Sometimes the *path* you need to take isn't clear,
the road you're on isn't marked
or signs aren't in the usual places.
Continuing on does not always seem
logical or practical.
But if your *heart* tells you
this is the way for you to go,
who has the right to deny you the *adventure*?
Traveling in a different direction
does not mean you are never coming back.
It may be a *change* of scenery
or it may *encourage* a lifelong
search for *beauty* and courage within you.
Couldn't we all use a little more of each
in our own lives?

What would it be
like to be a
snowflake?

Imagine yourself falling from
the sky to land with delicate
grace on the branch of a
pine. You may *believe* you
are merely a flake. If you were the
only one, you would soon melt and be a
moist reflection of what you used to be.
But when joined by others like you, you
become a *beautiful* picture worth
taking. When the time comes for you to
melt, you will quench the thirst of a tree
that beams green when the *world* is
thirsty for color. Sometimes we need
more flakes.

Bridges appear in places
where we sometimes wonder why they exist.
Is it to make the area more *beautiful*
or show the builder's talent?
Then one day it rains and
we must go to higher ground.
We realize this bridge is exactly
where we need it.
We see *life's waters flowing* beneath it.
Maybe constructing the bridge
was merely an artistic expression.
But now, this bridge is a road to safety.
Perhaps that is what art really is:
a bridge for some,
a way of life for others and
a direction toward which we all turn
when we need *peace*.

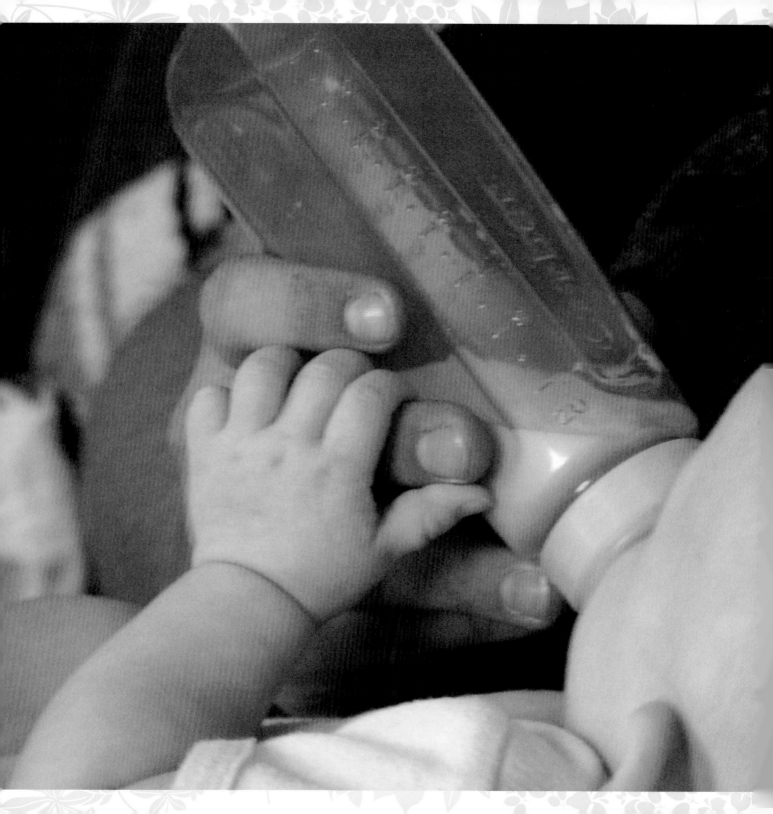

If I touch your *hand*,
your *heart*,
will you accept me as I grow
into the *person* I will become?
If I look at you with eyes
that see only you,
will you teach me to see the
world's goodness
through yours?
When I cry, will you comfort me,
say everything will be okay
and believe your own words?
Because you *love* me now,
will you *love* me later
when it is hard to know why I do what I do?
Because you take care of me when I am young,
may I take care of you when you're old?

Sometimes it feels as though
there's no one in the world except
you and me,
as if the only thing I need
to learn is how to find my way home.
The touch of your *hand* guides me,
teaching me that I don't have to pretend
I know where I'm going
or which road to take.
I just need to feel the
surface beneath my shoes and
take one step at a time
whether it be large or small.
Because, for now,
the most important thing is that we're
together and I don't have to know
what's around every bend.

There are days, weeks, months
when it feels as though there are
mountains all around:
mountains of bills,
mountains of pain,
mountains of *issues*.
It seems as though every envelope we open
or phone call we receive
is another *complication*.

Then, one day, we will find one
and know we do not have to conquer it,
at least not today,
not right now,
not this moment.
It will be one that is as *majestic*
as the rest but exists to be appreciated for its
beauty and does not need to be climbed.
Unless, of course,
you just want the exercise.

Let's disappear
to a deserted island.
Let's go where the world can't find us.
The complexities of life are piling up.
Let's shake them off and go stick our toes in the sand
and relax to the tune of the ocean's ebb and flow.
I will paint pictures,
and you can read books.
When the sun sets in the sky,
we'll judge our day's
accomplishments
by whether I found just the right color
and how far away your story took you.
As our time here ends,
we'll pack our things
and catch the next dolphin back to the
real world.

Do you remember the days of gazing at the sky
imagining what this cloud or that cloud looks like?
Did you find turtles, dragons, ice cream, Aunt Blanche?
What happened to those days?
Clouds are still there with all the makings of an imaginary figure.
Where are you?
Did you run out of time for such silly, childish games?
Are you as happy now as you were the day you and the other kid
saw the same thing in the same cloud?
Why wait any longer?
Grab a kid, no matter the age,
and remember the happiness clouds can bring.

Sometimes the road we're on
seems to have no end.
Just beyond it, all we see is a *mountain*.
It's then that we must *listen*
to the sound of our footsteps
and know we are moving forward.
This sound, of our own making,
is proof that we are taking ourselves beyond
our current circumstances.
Acknowledging the fact that this *bridge*
is strong enough to hold our weight
may not seem like much,
but some days having something that
will hold us up is all we need.
We can handle much more when we know
we have the *support* we need.

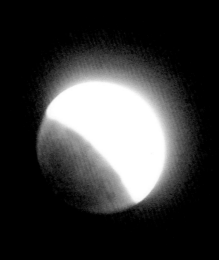

Life is an eclipse in progress.
It is a *wow experience* even in total darkness.
Like the moment the moon is covered
and can't be seen, observers stand mesmerized,
knowing it is there, knowing its rays will pour over
the night again.
Everyone watches.
This blackness cannot last.
But, what if it does?
What if the moon does not find its way
from behind the shadow?
Eyes watch as a sliver of white,
almost a dusty illusion appears and grows into a
brighter, stronger version of itself.
Those who watched helplessly *smile*,
appreciating more what they feared they had lost.

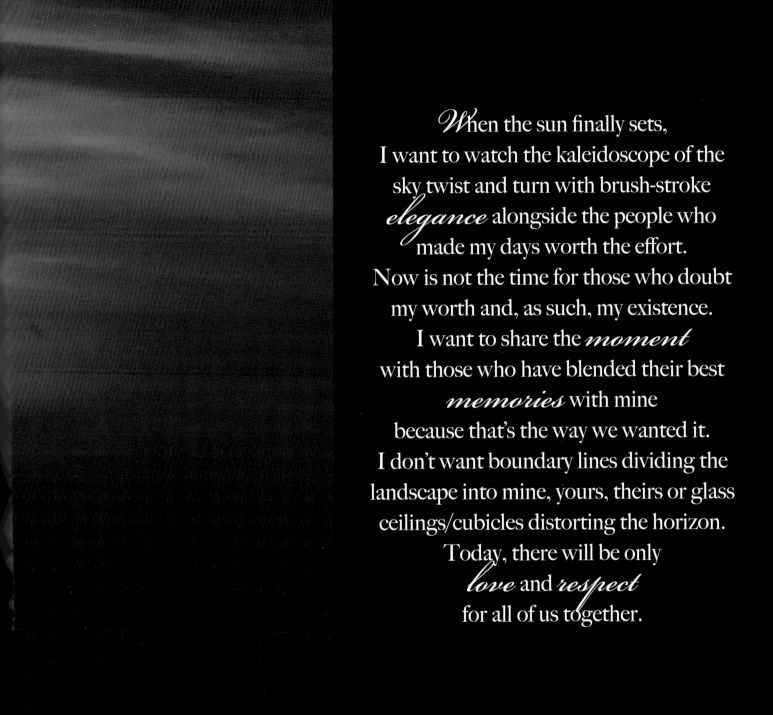

*W*hen the sun finally sets,
I want to watch the kaleidoscope of the
sky twist and turn with brush-stroke
elegance alongside the people who
made my days worth the effort.
Now is not the time for those who doubt
my worth and, as such, my existence.
I want to share the *moment*
with those who have blended their best
memories with mine
because that's the way we wanted it.
I don't want boundary lines dividing the
landscape into mine, yours, theirs or glass
ceilings/cubicles distorting the horizon.
Today, there will be only
love and *respect*
for all of us together.

Photo by Jessy Villarreal

ABOUT THE AUTHOR

Susan J. Mitchell

is a writer, poet and photographer from southeastern
Kentucky. Her photography is enjoyed in homes and
businesses in several states. The photos in this book were
taken in Kentucky, Michigan and Mexico.

You may visit Susan at **www.susanjmitchell.com**

You may visit Susan at

www.susanjmitchell.com